What's for Lunch?

Catherine Chambers

Contents

CAMBRIDGE
UNIVERSITY PRESS

UCL
Institute of Education

Time to stop for lunch!

All over the world, people take a break for lunch. Some go home to eat. Some take their own food to school or work. Others get a quick snack at a shop or a stall.

People are hungry and ready for something to eat by lunchtime. They need food that fills them up and gives them energy. That is why people often eat bread with their lunch.

Where does bread come from?

A long time ago, people found out that **grains** could be **ground** and made into flour. They used the flour to make bread.

Bread can be flat or thick, **crisp** or soft. People around the world make bread in different ways. Some people bake it in an oven and some people cook it in a pan.

people making bread in Ancient Egypt.

3

Lunch around the world

Bread is **vital** all over the world and is eaten with many dishes and fillings.

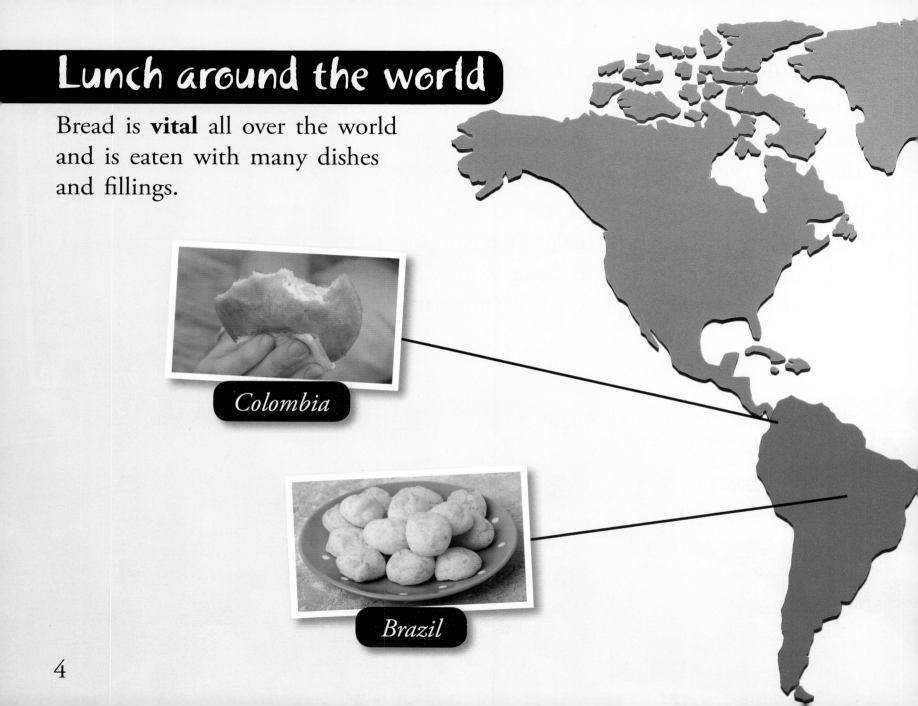

Colombia

Brazil

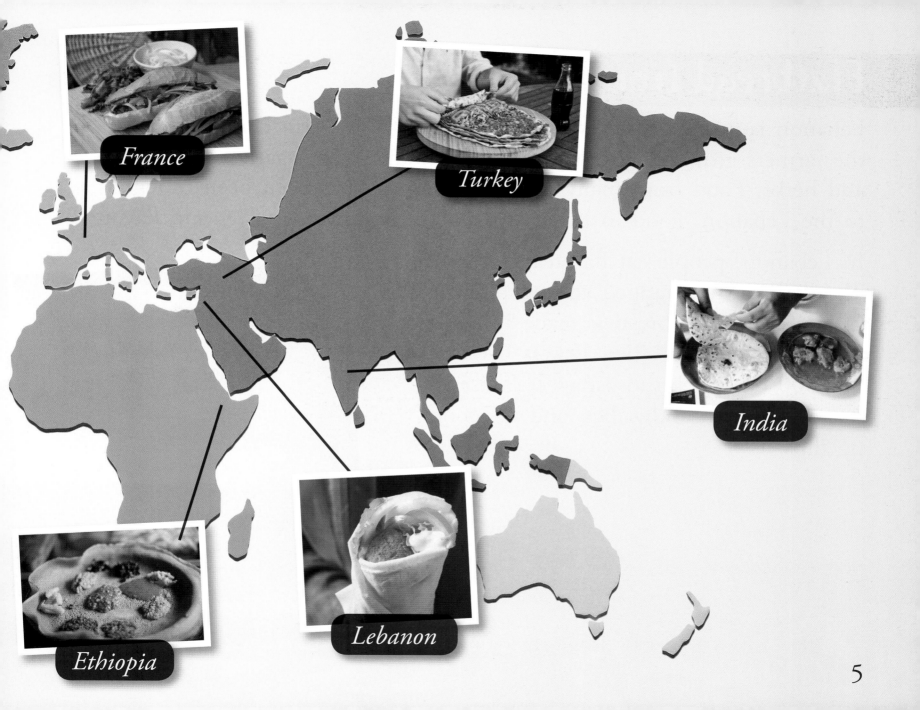

France

Turkey

India

Ethiopia

Lebanon

Flatbread from Lebanon

Lebanon is next to a sea with warm waters. The warm climate helps the farmers grow many crops, such as lemons, olives, garlic, grains and herbs. Food from many different countries has been been brought to the Lebanon. Food in Lebanon has lots of different tastes and flavours.

In Lebanon, people eat flatbread for lunch. The flatbread is wrapped around fillings, such as **falafel**. The flatbread is made in bakeries all over towns and cities. Bakers make almost 800,000 bags of bread a day. It is used to make delicious sandwiches, and to scoop up dips.

This man is making flatbread.

People go to special shops to buy their falafel. The falafel are wrapped in the flatbread. Pickles, salad and sauces can be added. People sometimes stay and eat the sandwich in the shop, and sometimes they take it away to eat.

*Falafel is a small **patty** made from beans and chick peas.*

Flatbread can be cooked on a very hot metal dome.

Lahmacun from Turkey

People from other countries moved into Turkey. They brought lots of different types of food with them. They liked their food to taste sweet and mild. Turkish food is spiced to add flavour.

Food was served on a huge, shiny, decorated metal tray called a sini.

Lahmacun is rolled thinly.

Lahmacun is a round, thin bread. It can be topped with minced meat, vegetables and spices. People make it at home, or buy it in a shop. It makes a filling and tasty lunch.

Lahmacun is often cooked in a wood-fired oven. This gives it a delicious, smokey flavour.

People put pickles, herbs and salad on the lahmacun. They then roll it up and eat it.

9

Roti from India

Farmers in the north of India grow vast fields of wheat. The wheat is ground into flour and made into a flatbread called roti. In India, people use roti to scoop up curry, pickles and salads. This makes a tasty and filling lunch.

People can buy roti from a bakery, but they often make their own roti at home. The dough is rolled out very thinly with a special rolling pin. The circle of dough is then cooked in a very hot pan.

People take lunch to work in a tiffin box. They eat their lunch with roti.

11

Injera from Ethiopia

Injera is a traditional spongy flatbread. It is used to soak up sauces and spicy stews. It is made from a small, round cereal called teff.

injera with toppings

Injera is not just the name of the bread. It is also the name of the spicy stew and the large metal dish it is served on. Injera is eaten with lots of different toppings: spiced bean stews, cabbage, chickpea sauces, meat and cheese. People sit around the dish and tear off a piece of the bread. They use it to scoop up the stews and sauces.

people enjoying injera

*The injera **batter** is poured quickly in a **spiral** from the outside inwards.*

13

Pao de queijo from Brazil

Pao de queijo is made from milk and cheese, mixed with cassava. People in Brazil eat cassava with many different meals.

Pae de queijo means 'cheese bread'. It is a small ball of cheesy bread that can be eaten as part of a lunch. It is also eaten as a snack, or even for breakfast.

Cassava grows under the ground. It looks like a sweet potato.

Pao de queijo breads are bought from bakeries, supermarkets and small, local shops. Some people make them at home.

freshly-cooked pao de queijo

It is very light and airy. People can eat several with their lunch.

Pao de queijo *has lots of holes.*

15

Arepa from Colombia

In Colombia, bread is made with cornflour. This flour is made by grinding dried corn. Corn is an important food because it keeps well over the winters when there is not much food.

Arepa are very tasty when eaten fresh from the grill or frying pan. They can be filled with eggs, cheese or meat. Arepa are often sold from stalls on the street. Shopkeepers grill these little breads in front of the customer.

The grill gives arepa lots of flavour.

Baguette from France

The baguette comes from France. Baguette means 'rod or baton', which is just what the bread looks like. A baguette has a soft inside and a crisp **crust** on the outside. People cut them in half and add tasty fillings.

These baguettes are being shaped.

People in France like to fill baguettes with cheese, eggs or meat. They also eat this bread with other meals. Baguettes are best eaten on the day they are made. People buy their bread every morning, to enjoy it when it is fresh.

French people travelled to other countries and took their favourite bread with them. Now, baguettes are enjoyed across the world. People choose what to fill the baguette with. For example, in Morocco, people fill baguettes with egg, salt, olive oil and cumin seeds.

Baguettes are sold all over the world.

19

Now you make a sandwich

You can use any bread you like to make a delicious sandwich. Roll the filling up in a Lebanese flatbread. Or put it in a French baguette. What other bread from the book would you like to try?

Try one of these fillings, or think of a sandwich you would like to make.

Cheese and cucumber

Ingredients

cheese slices

cucumber slices

lettuce

1 tablespoon mayonnaise

Method

Spread the mayonnaise on the bread.

Arrange cheese and cucumber slices on top.

Place lettuce leaves on top.

Tuna salad

Ingredients

can of tuna

a few salad leaves

1 teaspoon of olive oil

a squeeze of lemon juice

Method

Mix the tuna with the lemon and olive oil.

Put the salad leaves on the bread.

Spread the tuna mixture over the salad.

Hummus

Ingredients

4 tablespoons hummus

cucumber slices

tomato slices

a few salad leaves

Method

Spread the hummus on the bread.

Top with cucumber slices, tomato and salad leaves.

Cream cheese and jam

Ingredients

2 tablespoons cream cheese

2 tablespoons jam

Method

Spread the cream cheese on the bread.

Top with the jam, spreading carefully.

Glossary

bake	cook in an oven
batter	runny mixture
crisp	hard and crunchy
crust	outside of the bread
grains	seeds from grasses
ground	rubbed between two hard things to
patty	small roundish food
spiral	rounded shape that curves inwards
texture	way something feels
vital	very important

Index

What's for Lunch? — Catherine Chambers

Teaching notes written by Sue Bodman and Glen Franklin

Using this book

Developing reading comprehension

Bread, in some form or another, is a staple component of lunch in many regions of the world. This book explores different types of bread, looking at how these are combined with varied ingredients to make a delicious lunch for people to eat during a busy working day. Written predominantly as a non-chronological report, the book provides a secure model of this genre style, whilst including some reading of instructions as appropriate for children reading at White Band.

Grammar and sentence structure

- Sentence structures are longer, including multiple phrases or clauses, for example: 'People buy their bread every morning, to enjoy it when it is fresh.' (p.18).

- Grammar conventions clearly delineate the different text types, such as using a generic style and present tense verbs for non-chronological report, and imperative verbs for instructions.

Word meaning and spelling

- Place names and bread types provide opportunity to employ a range of reading strategies, including applying phonic knowledge, breaking into syllable chunks, and looking for known parts in reading unfamiliar words.

- Unfamiliar and technical vocabulary is supported by non-fiction features such as glossary definitions and additional information in captions and labels.

Curriculum links

Science – some breads are flat, whilst others are light and airy. Explore making bread with different rising agents such as soda and yeast.

Geography – bread is just one component of a healthy lunch. Children could explore another aspect of their own lunch, such as fruit, salad or drink, researching where these come from, and what is eaten or drunk with lunch in other countries.

Learning outcomes

Children can:

- recognise the features of non-fiction texts, and identify their different purposes

- search for and find information in texts, using these to demonstrate own understanding, orally and in writing

- use a range of strategies to read unfamiliar words and subject-specific vocabulary.

A guided reading lesson

Book Introduction

Give a copy of the book to each child. Ask them to read the title. Establish that this is a non-fiction book, asking children to name some of the features they would expect to see. Flick quickly through the book to check. Read the blurb to establish that the book is about a particular component of lunch – bread.

Orientation

Say: In this book, we are going to find out about the many different types of bread people around the world eat for lunch. If there a bread featured from your region, it might be helpful to start there to activate the children's prior knowledge. Look together at the map on pp.4-5 to see.

Preparation

Look at the first line on p.4 'Bread is vital all over the world'. Note the word 'vital' is in bold. Ensure the children are familiar with using a glossary, and discuss together the meaning of this opening sentence. Remind the children that non-fiction books are rarely read from cover to cover. Rather, they are for finding out specific information. Say: In this book, we can find out about different sorts of bread. Think of a purpose for why you might want to find out about a particular bread. For example, you could say: I am thinking of going to France to visit my uncle. I wonder what type of bread I might eat when I am there. Let's see.